Table of Content

MW01283529

Introduction

I'm just a Christian girl living in this crazy world. In this book, you as the reader will not only get to know me, but you will get a well-balanced mix of chapters surrounding my experiences, biblical knowledge, revelation, and inspiration. My goal is to give the reader a unique experience. I want you to feel like I'm right there with you, as you journey through each chapter. After each chapter, please take the time to reflect on everything you have learned and your process in each note section.

Let's get some of the instructions that I have for you out of the way, so that we are all on the same page. As I wrote the book and as I reflected on my life, **I highlighted every word/pattern that connected me to my childhood and my upbringing. Please feel free to do the same as you write in your reader's note sections. Once you reach the chapter titled "The power of words and how they can either heal or destroy," gather the words that you highlighted, good and bad, and then say a prayer releasing them.** Our goal is to embrace the positive words. Use one color to highlight the negative words and another color to represent the positive words. At the end of the book in the Reader's Journal section, take thirty days to reflect on what you have learned including the highlighted words, your wilderness process, your relationship with God, and your purpose.

Please note: This book is designed to be a guide during the process of finding your purpose and wilderness experience or past wilderness experience. So, it should be taken seriously for maximum results and it could take months to finish. We operate on God's timing. Please make your use of this book parallel to his plans for you. However, even if you aren't very religious but spiritual, or not in a season of finding your purpose, this book is still a great tool for encouragement, growth, and self-discovery. So let's get started, let me be the bridge that connects you to God and finding you purpose. Grab a coffee, grab a pen, and let's work out a plan to start changing your life with God at the center.

About the Author

Kristen Lory, is a woman of God, who wholeheartedly believes in Jesus and his word. Kristen has been a believer and an avid church goer for over 15 years. She is a wife and mother two children, and is currently a college student, and is studying to be a counselor. Kristen is completely overjoyed with the completion and early feedback of this guide. With this guide, Kristen hopes to help readers connect to God on a more intimate level, deal with and remove destructive patterns and strongholds, and ultimately unlock potential. On behalf of KDL Ministries, we hope you Enjoy!

WE WANT TO MEET YOU!!!

DO YOU WANT TO SHARE YOUR EXPERIENCE AND WHAT YOU HAVE

WRITTEN IN YOUR GUIDE?

IF YOU WANT TO BOOK ME AND MY TEAM (KRISTEN LORY MINISTRIES)

PLEASE EMAIL US AT Kloryfaithlovehope@gmail.com

WHETHER IT'S THROUGH YOUR CHURCH OR WITHIN A GROUP (AT LEAST

10 REGISTERED GUESS) GATHER YOUR PEOPLE AND WE WILL HANDLE THE REST.

LET'S COME TOGETHER AND TALK ALL THINGS HEALING AND PURPOSE

AND SHARE SOME OF WHAT YOU WROTE IN YOUR GUIDE!!

SEE YOU SOON!!!!

Me and You

Me

Ever since I was a child I knew that I wanted to be something more. I grew up as an only child, moved multiple times, attended several different schools, and made many friends along the way. However, I was a dreamer to say the least. There's a difference between dreaming through the eyes of an adult, versus the eyes of an adolescent child. As an adult, you've already experienced rejection and slammed doors. You've already been told that you can't do that, or that you might not be smart enough for that. When you're a child, anything is possible. The world seems safe, fair, and there are no limits. There's nothing like dreaming through adolescent eyes. But as the years pass and as we become adults, those dreams and those big bright eyes we once saw them through, get smaller and more practical. Why is that? I can honestly say, that it took me a while to find my purpose, as I struggled with my identity. Can you relate?

Despite my struggles, God just so happened to have blessed me with many gifts and talents, which we all have by the way. For example: I fell in love with music, writing, dancing, and singing. I found myself dabbling in every one of these areas throughout the years. But how do you begin to focus in on that one gift that God might be pressing on you? How do you begin to walk in your purpose? That was my issue. And to be frank I believe we all have this struggle. Here are some questions to ponder: Why do many of us settle for a life based on mediocracy? Is it fear? Perhaps not enough encouragement? Take some time to think about this.

In my thirty years of being on this earth I have met many people from diverse backgrounds. I have concluded that despite our many differences we all have one thing in common. We have all experienced Hurt. At some point in our lives, someone hurt us. Hurt can come from family, friends, significant others, people on the job, and strangers. By the time we enter college many of us will have already seen a counselor or a therapist. Some of us don't even make it to the couch, because our families may not believe in seeking outside help. Hurt is a very significant word, because it creates a scar that makes it difficult to experience life without bias. We become less trusting. We become more apprehensive. And it makes it hard for us to recognize the good things.

In my many attempts to find my calling in life, writing had seemed to stick out the most. Putting pen to paper came naturally, but finishing was always my greatest struggle. Once I had finally come to the realization that writing was the gift that God had blessed me with, I would begin what would turn out to be not only a long and drawn out arduous process, but one filled with many highs and lows, self-loathing, self-doubt, and serious writers block. Alright God, what do I write about now? Is it fiction? Or perhaps motivational? Should I write an autobiography? I had no idea of which way to start. After years of attempting each genre, failing miserably, and giving up about a million times, I finally found it. Not only did God want me to start my own ministry, but writing would be the premises of it all. When God began to press on me to start writing again, I wanted to give readers a personable, realistic, yet honest approach to finding one's purpose through God's eyes.

"Purpose Driven, Purpose Focused," is not only inspired by my own life journey and process, in the form of stories, ministry experiences, personal prayers, and a series of self-provoking questions, but I wanted readers to take a long and honest look at where they are today. Who are you? What do you think your life calling is? Candidly, have you asked God? Have you dealt with your mess along the way? What could be some roadblocks holding up your process or your next big breakthrough? And lastly, how and where does God fit into all of this? Never stop seeking the Lord and asking who you are in his eyes. I hope and pray that this not only helps you, but that it inspires you to get back up and take that leap of faith.

Prayer:

"Father God, give us the strength to acknowledge you always by keeping you first and giving you all of the glory. Lord, help us to climb up that mountain again. The enemy has tried to inflict us with fear, confusion, anxiety and doubt. We know that you have a plan and a purpose for our lives. Guide us, Oh Lord as we seek you and as we seek the call on our lives. Help us to take that leap of faith again. Amen."

Scripture of reference:

But scripture has locked up everything under the control of sin, so that what was promised, being given through faith in Jesus Christ, might be given to those who believe. (Galatians 3:22)

Reader's Notes: Take some time to tell me about you. List some of your greatest qualities. You deserve to be uplifted.

_____

_____

_____

_____

_____

_____

_____

_____

_____

_____

_____

_____

Geography

Community is key. Our past and the community that we grew up in affects who are as adults. Where you grow up and the circumstances surrounding that environment is detrimental to your growth. Sometimes, instead of looking at our partners or our friends for answers, we should be looking to our parents and who they were, when we were brought into this world, to get a better understanding of who we are as individuals. We pick up and inherit so much from our relatives, and I don't think we pay enough attention to that today.

My parents met at a party in the 80's. From what was told to me, they were both young and more into partying, having fun, and recreational drugs than each other. What they saw in each other besides an obvious physical attraction I don't know, but they couldn't have been any more different. My mother was born and raised to a widow and is one of five children. She was raised on an Indian reservation where poverty was at an all-time high and education was minimal. She was kind of the black sheep of the family, a role I would eventually find myself in as I got older. My mother was tough to say the least. Everybody knew when she was in the room. Known to be a dreamer, her goal was to always be better than her circumstances. Unfortunately, having a child wasn't apart of those dreams but I came into the world anyway.

My father on the other hand was much more intricate. He grew up different from my mother. Along with his brother, my father grew up in a working-class home with two working parents. My father and his brother were spoiled. They had everything they wanted, from motorcycles to fancy clothes and more. Maybe when my mother realized that my dad lived this kind of life it spiked a deeper interest.

My grandmother (my father's mother) died in a car accident right before I was born. My father wanted to name me after her (Sandra) but my mother said no, breaking my father into pieces. Instead, she opted to name me Kristen, after watching a daytime soap opera. My father would go on to struggle his whole life. He lied, went to prison and battled addiction. Eventually, he got married and gave me my half siblings, but he lived a hard life. I would say that having me was his first great decision, then meeting and marrying my stepmother was his second. Despite my father's run-ins with the law, he has always been faith based.

After my birth, my father didn't believe that I was his. He came to the hospital with his baby picture and once he saw me he instantly knew that I was his. My mother, being the stubborn woman that she is, provoked the situation by saying "You could be right!" They fought over everything. Despite their madness which involved many arguments, fights, my mother stealing my dad's car and motorcycle trying to be cool, and many other adventures, they did try to make it work and stayed together up until I was about three. My father told me that once my mother told him to leave after an explosive argument, he left and walked away for good. After that, I would only see my father once or twice a year if I was lucky. There you have it. My first experience with "Hurt". Geography huh?

Prayer:

Lord, I may never understand why certain things in the past have happened or what your reasoning were behind them, but despite it all I am grateful for my parents and that 80's party that united them. Please Lord, give me the strength to forgive and forget and to know that I was not an accident but a part of an intricate design. Apart of your creation. apart of Your masterpiece. Amen!

Scripture of reference:

Children, obey your parents in the Lord, for this is right. "Honor your father and mother"—which is the first commandment with a promise "so that it may go well with you and that you may enjoy a long life on the earth." (Ephesians 6)

Fathers, do not exasperate your children; instead, bring them up in the training and instruction of the Lord. (Ephesians 6)

Reader's Notes: Reflect on your childhood. Reflect on how your parents met and the environment at that time. Do you notice any patterns so far?

_____

_____

_____

_____

_____

_____

_____

_____

_____

_____

_____

_____

_____

God as I Know Him

If someone were to ask me if I had any regrets in my life, despite all the highs and lows, I would honestly have to say no. I think the real question would be whether I regret not keeping God at the center of it all. Of course my answer would be YES! I made it a point to start the chapter off like this because I want you as the reader to sit back and really think about your life. Go back into time. Think about relationships. Think about the good moments and think about the bad. Think about all the defining moments in your life. Think about all of your brokenness, your hurt and your pain. Be it past or present. Now think about the goodness of our Lord and Savior and how much he loves us and then let it go! Release it! If you must cry, then cry! If you must scream then scream! But whatever happens, no matter how hard it is, release the pain and let it go!

You must do the work. It's not easy dredging up painful memories, but my friend this is what will free you. You must think about the time you had an eating disorder, or the time he hit you. The time you were raped. The time you were molested. Lied to. Lost a loved one. Or the time you may have caused the hurt to someone else. People don't want to talk about the challenging times, but instead will suppress it, causing us to walk in this silent and invisible bubble filled with guilt and shame. This gives the enemy dominion over our lives and pushes God further and further away. Our God is a loving and merciful God. Do the initial work and the not so easy remembering and he will heal you. He will set you free.

Many of us today, including myself, have been operating from a place of brokenness. Whether we grew up in an abusive situation or endured poverty or hardship, it has in some way or another shaped who we have become. This of course, has impacted God's ability to really move in our lives, preventing us from living it abundantly while interfering with our purpose. That's why so many of us are lost. We don't have a clue as to who we really are. And as a society we are wondering why suicide and depression are at an all-time high. People feel like they don't fit in, like they don't have a purpose here on this planet when in fact they do. We all do! you do!

But God is good right? You don't have to be another statistic. You don't have to go down that road everybody else is traveling. I call it the road of carnality. See, God has a specific and predestined road for each and every one of us. We don't have to be a victim to our circumstances. We can live the most abundant and fruitful life, if we get real with ourselves, instead of covering our imperfect lives with the makeup of this world. (money, fame, materialistic things) Instead, we should be taking the time to get to know our Lord and Savior.

So what is it really like being a Christian woman today? When you're a child your knowledge of the Father, Son and the Holy Spirit rests on your surroundings, be it your immediate family or the church you attend and its denomination. I always thought that my relationship with God was determined by my praise or how loud I could shout in church. But over the years, I have learned that those loud shouts in church hardly scratch the surface when it comes to an authentic relationship with the Lord. And a lot of times, the main ones shouting in church usually are the ones doing the most dirt. Are you a shouter? Are you an authentic believer?

Our relationship with God is not determined by our successes whether it be in love, marriage, career, or finances. Yes, God wants us to increase in these areas but it's our salvation, treatment toward others, and that inner peace that He cares about the most. Our biggest example would be the Apostle Paul. After his name change (Saul to Paul), did he have money? Did he have a mansion? Did he even own multiple outfits? Most of the time the bible talks about his imprisonment throughout his ministry, but despite his lacking he had an inner peace. He was closer to God than ever before. Are you willing to ask God to change your name? Would you allow Him to make you over by transforming your mind and healing your soul?

Prayer:

"Dear Lord, we know that we are a mess. Father God we know that we are not worthy of your mercy and grace, yet you give it to us anyway. Please make us brand new Father God. Transform our minds, our heart and our souls. Heal our brokenness oh Lord, so that we can live life not only with you at the center but to live it as fruitful and as abundantly as possible. Amen!"

Scripture of reference:

"See now that I, myself am he! There is no God besides me; I kill, and I make alive; I wound and I heal; and there is none that I can deliver out of my hand." (Deuteronomy 32:39)

Reader's Notes: What would your name change be? What would that look like? How would this change you?

_____

_____

_____

_____

_____

_____

_____

_____

_____

_____

_____

_____

_____

_____

_____

_____

Seasons of Embarrassment

You went to church last Sunday and you told the Lord that you were ready to change your life (for real this time.) Well now it's Tuesday and you're already cursing out the fast food worker at the drive through, or your spouse for not picking up their dirty laundry. Your man or woman asks you for some nude photos and you know you should say no but because you're feeling sexy and the impulse is there, you send them anyway. Or you find yourself in the middle of that heated argument and you know you shouldn't hit the send button or tell them to stick it where the sun doesn't shine but you do it anyway. We all have moments like this. We have moments, or seasons where we just aren't there, or were we suffer from some embarrassing moments. To be honest, I might have some nude photos out there somewhere. That was before my name change. Ha!

But my point is that it's alright! God doesn't expect us to be perfect, but He expects us to mature and to do away with the things of our youth. He understands our flesh and how much of a hindrance it can be. He understands that we have an adversary who's out to destroy us at every turn. Being a believer is about endurance and perseverance. God honors this. As believers we are already given salvation through our Lord and Savior. The only thing that will land you into the lake of fire is blasphemy of the Holy Spirit, not believing that Jesus is the way to the Father, and continual sin. If we avoid such avenues we are safe. Not to say that we have no worries, but the Lord wants to save the world not condemn it. There is much that goes into our salvation and God's process. In the meantime, do some research on the Ten Commandments and read up on continual sin and read revelations.

Prayer:

"Father God, please give me the ability to not walk in shame. I know that I have walked in some seasons where I wasn't on my best behavior, and where I did not put you first, which caused some embarrassment and shame. But Father God, I now wholeheartedly serve you. I am a representative of who you are. Please help me Lord to bless, release, and move forward."

Scripture of reference:

And Now, little children, abide in him so that when he appears we may have confidence and not hide from him in shame at his coming. (1 John 2:28)

Reader's Notes: Talk about one of your most embarrassing moments and what it has taught you. Write it down and tell me all about it.

_____

_____

_____

_____

_____

_____

_____

_____

_____

_____

_____

_____

_____

Dad

Dear Dad,

I believe we are very similar. I believe we both have the same heart. I believe we both love God. I believe we both love affection and attention. We have the same eyes. We have the same "it's all about me" trait and I believe deep down inside, despite the rough edges, we have good intentions. I think it's cool that we both have our own ministries. You are currently in jail, this time for something very minor, but I'm sure you are teaching the gospel.

After all these years I finally have the courage to tell you how I feel. I have the courage to tell you the truth. My mother use to say to me "why aren't you mad at him? Why do I get the crappy end of the stick when he's always welcomed with open arms?" I guess it's because I always understood you. Honestly you were always gone, so not having you around hardly affected me until I started noticing boys.

I think what it really came down to is the fact that I never really had a voice. I mean as a child our wants and opinions are limited anyway. But growing up with a mother who made it clear that her way was the law, I couldn't exactly say how I felt regardless. But the truth is I can't hold it in anymore. I can't fix me without fixing my issues with you. It's now or never.

Dad, when I was about twelve, I remember going shopping with a childhood friend and her father. I remember the conversation that her mother and father had regarding him taking us both, and to be honest I didn't know what to expect. Why not? Because I didn't know what that looked like. I don't even recall us ever going out anywhere in public prior to my older years. Anyways, so my friend's father came to pick us up in his nice car and we were off to buy my friend some clothes. After walking through the mall and stopping and looking at different clothing, we had finally found a couple of shirts that my friend liked, "Well, what shirt do you want Amanda?" said her father, as he pointed off to the shirts in front of us. I remember just staring at him. He was tall, he was handsome, and he was patient. My friend and I had run off a couple of times and instead of yelling he smiled and waved an (alright girls come on now) type of wave.

He was very gentle with us and he made us laugh. Now I don't know if it was God or if it was just coincidence, but as he took my friend up to the counter to pay for her shirt, he looked back at me and said "Hey, do you want a shirt too?" My face lit up and I said yes. He walked over toward me and said, "Come on, let's pick something out," and I did. It was a red and white striped shirt, I wore it so much that it fell apart. But besides not feeling left out, to this day, I still remember how it made me feel. To have a "dad" even if he wasn't mine, give me that moment, to show me what a father was like even if it wasn't permeant, was wonderful and a moment I'll never forget. Thank you anonymous "Father." But dad, it was moments like that and other similar moments throughout the years, that made me miss you the most.

I was fine when I was home and just living life without you, but during those moments with anonymous "fathers," I really wished you were around and wanted to cry out to you the most. But I understand dad that life got the best of you. Your story is your own story. We can't change the past. We can't change what happened. But we can start opening up and telling the truth. I do appreciate the past couple of years. We got to talk, we spent time, we laughed. You got to see your grandchildren again and for that I am thankful. I forgive you and I love you dad.

Love Always,

Kristen

Prayer:

"Father God give me the strength to forgive my dad and to move on. Help me to heal oh Lord as I navigate through the dark times. I know you can restore it all Lord. Thank you for the past couple of years that my father and I have had, but it wasn't enough to heal me. I must tell him the truth. Please give me the strength to do so. Amen!"

Scripture of reference:

As a father has compassion on his children, so the Lord has compassion on those who fear him. (Psalm 103:13)

Mom

Dear Mom,

I believe we are both very similar. You always hated when I made comparisons between us two, but there are some things that we simply cannot avoid. I would call our relationship precarious to say the least. Although there have been many tears and many ups and downs, I will never neglect the good moments we shared. You gave me my first credit card, you gave me my first car and you showed me what hard work looked like as a business woman. Mom, most importantly, you taught me how to not give up, even when people have wronged you along the way.

I always heard this saying about how children see their parents as superheroes. I see this with my own children as I navigate through the passages of being a parent. Mom, you were my hero once. I wouldn't classify our relationship as a traditional parent and child relationship. Things that other families deemed important like affection, saying I love you, or cooking dinner every night weren't a priority. Despite the pain you have caused me and despite the storms, your role as my mother never changed and your light never faded.

When I was in middle school, I remember having this feeling of certainty about you. Whenever we walked into a store or into a nice restaurant, I knew that money would never be an issue. You always seemed to have it together all the time. I even recall watching you in the bathroom as you put on your makeup and curled your hair. Back then I was just a tomboy, but I still remember saying to myself, "wow, I wish I was as beautiful as my mom." Whether it was an outfit, or styling your hair, you always seemed to do things in a way I could never do them. I thought you were perfection.

Despite our turbulent relationship, I always wanted to impress you and make you proud the most. Whether it was speaking French to you, or showing off good grades in Global Studies, I wanted you to be proud of me. I wanted you to believe in me. When I felt like you didn't believe in me, when the desire to show you my French homework or my good grades stopped, something in me changed forever. If I couldn't make you happy, or if I could not make you proud, what was the point of it all?

At nineteen, I decided to mother my own child, in hopes of getting that desire to do better and to be better again. I don't have much to say, for if I continue, it might not be too good. I hope one day we can find common ground and mend a relationship that has been filled with scars, tears, battles, and resentment. I forgive you for everything that has happened. I hope that you can forgive me too for anytime I might have been disrespectful. I have chosen to let go of the anger, I have chosen to forgive and to let God do his work for us. I am ready when you are.

Sincerely,

Kristen

Prayer:

"Father God give me the strength to fully forgive my mother and to move on. Help me to heal oh Lord, as I navigate through the dark times. I know you can restore it all Father God. Thank you for the good moments that my mother and I have had. Help us to heal from years of turbulence and hurt oh Lord. There is nothing that you can't do. I will continue to praise you. Amen!

Scripture of reference:

Train up a child in the way he should go; even when he is old he will not depart from it. (Proverbs 22:6)

Readers Notes: Write a letter to your parents telling them how you felt during a particular time they hurt you. Tell your truth.

_____

_____

_____

_____

_____

_____

_____

_____

_____

_____

_____

_____

_____

_____

_____

_____

Dealing with the Unexpected and Pinpointing the Start of Brokenness

When we think of the word broken, we often associate it with an item of some sort. But I don't think we ever truly pay it enough attention when it comes to our lives. A lot of times, many of us don't even know that we have it. My brokenness stems from my relationships with the people who raised me, having a child at the age of twenty and losing my grandmother. My grandparents raised me from the time I was about three, up until my grandmother's passing. My grandfather eventually moved to the south but continues to be a father figure in my life to this day. So if anybody knows what the word failure means it's me. I wasn't always purposed driven. I didn't always have a consistent relationship with God. And it took me a while to get a good footing in life. It took a lot of work and a lot of Jesus to get to where I am today.

Becoming a young mom, wasn't exactly apart of my plan. After seeing friends and relatives experience motherhood at a young age, and the drama that came with it, I told myself that would never be me. But unfortunately I became another statistic anyway. The relationship with my daughter's father was very tumultuous, abusive and toxic. After multiple fights, calls to the police, trips to family court, bruises, crying, and depression, I had finally had enough. I thought to myself, I am so much more than this. I would find myself in the mirror saying, why are you doing this to yourself? Take a stand! Push yourself! Fight smart! Stop fighting this guy and fight the enemy! So after six years it all ended. To this day it's still a work in progress, but I thank God for the progress that has been made thus far.

Going back to when I was pregnant, my grandmother was a constant support for me right up until my daughter's birth. Unfortunately, right after my daughter turned one, my grandmother passed on. I was completely and utterly devastated. I ended up falling into a deep and dark depression and I dropped out of college. I never allowed myself to fully deal with her death. I just held it in. But I remember one night having a dream of her telling me to go back to school. I believe, that it was God, using her in that dream as a way of telling me to pull myself together and to get back up. See, the Lord will do that. He lives inside of us and knows us better than we know ourselves. He tends to use our own voice, personality, and life attachments to communicate with us.

My grandmother was a huge mother figure in my life. Aside from her, there were a handful of other women who were like mother figures to me as well. Due to confidentiality purposes, I will refer to a particular woman as one of my "Mother Figures." This particular "mother figure" and myself, had a very interesting relationship that only became more toxic and abusive as I got older. As you may recall, my father was an absent father who struggled with addiction, so naturally I hardly saw him, and my biological mother eventually faded into the background. So these relationships, the most important relationships in my life, were the first examples of what love looked like and what heartache felt like.

When Hurricane Sandy hit, she didn't just hit long island, she hit my life too. My life was literally a mess. I was a single mother and a full-time college student. But after a year of living on campus, my mother figure, began having financial difficulties with her home. After having a discussion with her, she had convinced me to move in with her and I had stupidly taken a leave of absence from college just to help with the bills. I did not pray about this, nor did I ask God. But to make a long story short, I ended up owing the college money. Not doing my homework, I mistakenly withdrew from the semester too early and I never went back. This led to me being penalized financially. Not even a month later, I had found myself kicked out of a home with my child, with no place to go over a dispute and I had become more depressed than ever before.

I know what being homeless looks like. I know what living in and out of your car looks like. I know how it feels to not have a place to call your own. Back then, I know people wondered about me, when they would see me for a few months and then suddenly I'd be gone. People would see me in church and then I would disappear. I had taken on this nomadic lifestyle. A nomadic lifestyle equals an inconsistent lifestyle. I began living life on the road, trying to survive and stay afloat, all while trying to raise my daughter. Making sure she ate had become my life's motto. These were some of the most painful and most embarrassing moments of my life. During those times I blamed myself completely and every single word that was said to me, every act of abuse that was put on me, I thought I deserved it.

During those times God was silent. When I look back, I know it was for the purpose of teaching me, developing me, and molding me into the woman and Christian I am today. Not once did I ever doubt God. Not once did I ever turn away from him. I knew He wasn't being mean, but sometimes suffering is necessary. Would I have written this book if I had not experienced such pain, a pain that connects me to you and millions of other people around the world? I would have to say no. If it had not been for such a painful process, I would not be the woman I am today. Later in life, I would come to find out that it was because of the call on my life that God lead me down a path of such adversity. But he never left me completely hanging either. During those times I really had to lean on him.

Once that season came to an end, finally, the Lord began speaking to me and it was incredible! All of those little things that I heard in my head throughout the years, and all of those gut feelings finally started making sense. Suddenly his voice became louder. He came with warnings, and he came with a plan. A plan that seemed so far-fetched, but it would change my life forever. The Lord began telling me to leave. He told me loud as day to get up and go. I asked why? He told me that it was the only way and so I left. I left everything behind. The Lord promised that I would get it all back and with interest.

When God tells us to do something it can be scary, Often times when he comes with a plan, the enemy is ready to cast fear. The enemy will always try to silence you and cause you to walk in condemnation. The enemy begins to use this, as not only a license (we talk about this later), but as ransom over our heads to keep us separate from God. Before you know it, you begin to walk through life wearing all of this, along with all the other baggage you chose to carry, because you didn't fully know or understand God and his role in our lives. God wants you to use that story to tell others so that they too can see how he healed you. He wants to do the same for them as well.

Prayer:

"Father God, heal us and help us to release every single hurt, grudge, pain, and every time someone has harmed us. We want to move forward in life oh Lord. We want to give you the glory oh Lord. We want to tell others what you have done for us so that they too can give you their burdens. You are Alpha and Omega. The beginning and the end. We give you the glory Lord. Amen!"

Scripture of reference:

For this reason, also, since the day we heard of it, we have not ceased to pray for you and to ask that you may be filled with the knowledge of His will in all spiritual wisdom and understanding. (Colossians 1:9)

Reader's Notes: When did your first experience with brokenness happen and with whom? Have an honest moment with yourself, address your brokenness head on and then release it.

_____

_____

_____

_____

_____

_____

_____

_____

_____

_____

_____

_____

_____

_____

_____

Secrets, Regrets, Apologies, and Forgiveness

This is probably the most difficult and most controversial chapter in this book. I did not include this part in the chapter on brokenness because I felt it needed a chapter of its own. I also know that this is a major issue in our communities, in our families, and in our own homes. The issue at hand is sexual harassment and all of its various forms. It also took me a while to muster up the courage to even speak about it. But I have to tell my truth. Life is too short and because of everything that we have been discussing thus far, I had to reach into that secret space and release what has been haunting me for so long.

When I was younger I was sexually harassed and inappropriately touched by family members, and this scarred me and confused me. Growing up I wasn't sure about my sexuality because of what had happened to me. I could never tell my story to my immediate family. It took a couple of my other cousins going through the same experiences for me to finally tell the truth. This story is so much bigger than just me and involves so many other people besides me. But it is up to them to want to speak up and tell their truth. I believe that as a family, we all need to come together and have an honest conversation about things that have happened to us when we were younger, so we can move forward, forgive one another, love one another, and to stop the cycle. It is never too late. I just want to add that I love all of my family members dearly.

My experiences with sexual harassment added to the depression in my life, it led to many poor choices, and the hurting of others. It is truly a cycle that gets passed down from one generation to another. As a child you do not have the ability to decipher right from wrong. As a learned behavior what you think is normal, appropriate, and just, is distorted by what you yourself experienced and was taught. I have made peace with it all. I have forgiven those who have hurt and wronged me. I apologize to those whom I have hurt and wronged due to situations beyond my control. I have given it to God. I have made amends. I have been forgiven and I have been healed.

She no longer has anything to hide, nor anything to keep the enemy knocking. I made it! And it's all because of God. Do not let secrets hold you back. Secrets are dangerous, they are like anchors and they can hold us down forever. Some people even believe that just because they did that one thing, be it the accused or accuser, life is over. But the truth is that it's not. Besides kindness, and love, we owe nothing to nobody, only to God. In the long run we must answer to him. Many things happen in our pasts that contribute to our mistakes. It's your salvation on the line, make amends today!

I will never publicly shame or out anyone. Many of them know who they are. I forgive them all and I love them all. I ask anyone else whom I might have hurt to forgive me as well. I have made peace with all my doings and I have given them all to God. There's no need to let situations control me any longer or to guilt me. Will you do the same? I decided not to carry around anymore secrets, will you do the same?

Check in Time: You have been doing great. At this point, not only have you learned a lot about me, but you have been doing the inner work for you. You've dug deep into your past and into your pain. You've acknowledged some things I'm sure you never even knew existed. But you made it to this point, you are almost there. Now it's time to face that person, place, thing, or addiction this one final time. Address it head on and then let's get into your purpose.

_____

_____

_____

_____

_____

_____

_____

_____

_____

_____

_____

_____

Prayer:

"Lord give me the strength to forgive my enemies and the people who hurt me. I will not give anymore power to that person or that thing. It was a part of my past and the person I used to be. Father you have made me brand new. Please continue to heal me Lord so I can move on and live a healthy life in peace. Goodbye brokenness! Hello Happiness! Amen!"

Scripture of reference:

"Have compassion on me, Lord, for I am weak. Heal me, Lord, for my bones are in agony." (Psalm 6:2)

Reader's Notes: Are you ready? Address the abuser right now. Address that molester. Address the eating disorder, Address the rapist. If you're the wrongdoer, Address it, Repent it, and Release it.

_____

_____

_____

_____

_____

_____

_____

_____

_____

_____

_____

_____

_____

Write A Letter to The Younger You. What Advice Would You Give Your Younger Self?

A Healthier You

Ever since I turned thirty I realized the importance of self-care. It is true. As you get older there are some things that you just can't do anymore. For example; staying up for twenty-four hours straight, hanging at the clubs all night long, or drinking yourself into oblivion, just won't make the cut anymore. Our bodies change and we no longer process things the same. There are even some people who can't eat sweets after a while. Others can no longer drink coffee. And the list goes on and on. I want to take the time to encourage you right now to live a healthier life. Your body is a temple. It will take care of you if you take care of it. It took me a long time to understand this, but when minor health issues began popping up, I knew that I had to make a change.

It doesn't help that most of our foods are processed and that our country does a poor job of labeling and monitoring where our food comes from. So it's important that we become more conscious of what we eat and drink. I recently started drinking apple cider vinegar. I do that in moderation with a cup of warm water and honey. I also take supplement powder, which consists of super foods like: ginger, wheatgrass, kale, spinach, and barley grass. If you want to move forward in life and in your purpose you must have the energy. You must take care of yourself.

Prayer:

Father God, please give me the ability to be more conscious of what I put into my body. I know that my body is my temple and that I must be ready and fully energized. Lord I thank you Amen.

Scripture of reference:

Worship the Lord your God, and his blessing will be on your food and water. I will take away sickness from among you. (Exodus 23:25)

Readers Notes: Write down your eating habits. What does your diet look like and how can you change it? How can you honor your body?

_____

_____

_____

_____

_____

_____

_____

_____

_____

_____

_____

_____

Love/Marriage

I have heard people say that marriage is one of the hardest things that we will ever do. Do you believe that saying? Can I be honest? Not only did I not get this sentiment, but I also never knew what it truly meant until I married my husband. Marriage is hard. Let me be redundant, marriage is extremely hard. It literally is a choice that we are choosing to make every single day with that person. Marriage is not for the faint of hearts. Our marriage covenant with our spouse is like the covenant between the Lord and his church. It shall not be divided. Let's talk about the word divided. The enemy loves the word "divide" and he also likes the word "conquer," especially when it pertains to marriage. Therefore, we must keep God at the center of our unions to preserve it.

Never in my life have I ever had to compromise so much or put someone else's needs before mine. I was never good at being the bigger person and taking the high road but being married has taught me how to do just that. Can I be honest again? There were times when I despised my husband. There were times where I couldn't even look at his face. You go through such an emotional rollercoaster ride. Sometimes you are on this high and then you hit a low. You go through seasons of wonderful and then you find yourself sleeping in the room downstairs or separated. How else can I explain this? I can't!

Put your socks away. Please, put your dirty clothes in the hamper. Get your snoring checked out. Why can't you listen to me? Why don't you touch me like you used to? I don't want to watch that movie again. Your gas smells bad. I love you soo much babe. Thank you for the flowers. That movie was great. Should I get lingerie? Don't even think about touching me. More kids? Alright one more kid. I mean this is what happens daily. The list really goes on and on. But that is the beauty of it all. These are the moments that count, be it good or bad. Everything is meant to help us grow closer as a union.

I just wanted to encourage all married couples. Especially married couples who are believers. Even if you aren't married but you have been with someone for a long time, I know you can relate. Don't give up. Learn how to put your pride to the side and see things from his or her perspective. Do the inner work that might be required for you to be a better partner. Don't just pick at what they do or don't do. Try listening. Keep dating each other. Marriage is truly wonderful. It is never the marriage that's the problem, but the individuals involved, who need to do the inner work.

I also wanted to talk about the pressure that is put on us as married couples in the church. God hates divorce. Because of this scripture, it has been ingrained in our heads that if we leave a marriage we could possibly go to hell. Many leaders have their own opinions on this topic, but the word is the word at the end of the day. I happen to believe that everything is circumstantial. God deals with us differently as our own unique individual. He knows the type of heart we have. He knows when we have done all that we could to make the marriage work. If you have tried everything from prayer, to counseling, to sitting with your pastor, to temporary separations, and any other methods to help preserve the marriage, and still nothing has worked, then you should go to God with a heart of repentance and pray to Him for guidance on how to leave.

This chapter on marriage is very important because today in the church and in ministry, we have so many couples living in secret misery. The enemy has defiled their marriage bed with adultery, lies and deceit. We want to hold onto our titles, so therefore we condone our partners cheating ways and behaviors. This is a huge issue in the church. A lot of times, these are the couples in ministry. These are the couples that you look up to and aspire to be like. These are the musicians, singers, prophets and psalmists. Nobody is perfect, but if you have been called to a certain ministry, God holds you to a certain level of accountability and expects us to lead exemplary lives. Do what's right. Don't listen to people in the church regarding your marriage.

Don't let titles keep you in a dead-end marriage that could cost you your salvation. Even if you aren't the cheating partner, just knowing what he or she is doing and by not doing anything to remedy the situation with God, holds you just as equally as responsible. God sees the individual but also sees the union. Two are now joined as one and we must pray for our partners in their time of need and when they are weak. If you've tried your best and it isn't working or if your partner refuses to fix their wrongdoings, let it go and let God deal with it. There is someone out there for you who can add to your life and your purpose.

A Tip from Me to you:

Make sure you know who you are and what you have been called to do before you marry your future husband or wife. I am not saying that your marriage won't work if you don't do this, but I am saying that you can save yourself and your partner a lot of unnecessary stress if you do so. What if your partner doesn't want to be in ministry? What if your partner doesn't want to support your vision? These are important topics to deal with and to discuss when dating a potential spouse before you say I do.

Prayer:

(You fill out this one)

_____

_____

_____

_____

_____

_____

Scripture of reference:

He who finds a wife finds what is good and receives favor from the Lord. (Proverbs 18-22)

Readers Notes: Take a moment to give thanks to your partner. Instead of focusing on the negative build on the positive. If you are divorced, write about forgiveness and some of the positive things that came out of that Union and what you learned about yourself!

_____

_____

_____

_____

_____

_____

_____

_____

_____

_____

_____

_____

_____

_____

Life is More Than Just a Hashtag

When some people look at me I know they see a strong beautiful woman who is a mother, wife, and a Jesus lover. And although this may be true, it wasn't always the case. When I was in high school and right up until my twenties, pictures became a way of life. Social media began taking off and before I knew it I had about four social media profiles. It was literally like a job to post daily and to stay up to date. When I look back at that person, I see a girl who was lost. I see a woman who needed salvation.

The infamous "selfie" was a way to feel full even though I was empty. I believe that everybody in this world has some type of a void from that time they got hurt. We all take to social media to feel a little better about ourselves. We love to mask the pain instead of confronting it. I can't tell you how many friends of mine put on a show by posting pictures just to create a phony image and a false reality. We need validation from other people. We need to see the likes, and love, and funny emojis. But really all we need at the end of the day is our Lord and savior. He is the only one who can truly fill us up.

Now that I am thirty and have been healed and freed from many, or just about all the demons from my past, I am no longer that girl who looks for validation every minute from some stranger on some social media site. Remember that you are worth more! Remember that you are truly loved by your friends, family, children, spouse, and God. You don't need the rest of the world to tell you what you already know, and that is that you are beautiful. I was never able to show my skills, be it writing, singing, or dancing, or teaching, because those things were meant to happen later in my life, but I will show everybody that despite my late start in life, I am more than just a face and some social media hashtags. Your turn!

Prayer:

Dear Lord, help me to block out the distractions. Help me to see past the mirror and to focus on you. I am more than just a face. I am smart. I am educated. And there are many things I would love to accomplish with your help and guidance. Lord I know that I post a lot of selfies on social media, and I know that I gossip, but that is because I am empty in an area of my life. Release me oh Lord from this nationwide problem of your children, thinking that they need validation from social media and others. Amen!

Scripture of reference:

"For I am now seeking the approval of man, or of God? Or am I trying to please man? If I were still trying to please man, I would not be a servant of Christ" (Galatians 1:10)

Readers Notes: It took me a long time to feel confident. It took me a while to realize that I don't need anybody's validation. Write down your stance on social media and how it makes you feel? Does it feel good to post frequently or could you care less? Do you seek the approval of others?

_____

_____

_____

_____

_____

_____

_____

_____

_____

_____

_____

_____

_____

_____

A Moment of Reflection: Was there ever a time where you had to prove that you were more than just a (Fill in the blank)?

_____

_____

_____

_____

_____

_____

_____

_____

_____

_____

_____

_____

_____

_____

_____

_____

To the Man Who Dreams of Dying on the Street

When I was working for a shelter, I came across many interesting people, some with very interesting stories. The more I got to know these individuals the more I realized they are just like me and you. Some people were frequent shelter goers, and were the ones who came back every year. There were the people that got into trouble and had to be there. There were some who just couldn't get ahead in life, and then there were some who enjoyed shelter life. I will never forget the man who told me he had dreams of dying on the street.

This gentleman was unlike anybody I had ever met. He said he was a "Tramp" someone who lives life camping, and travelling, and prefers not to have any belongings beyond a few items. He was very quiet, he stayed to himself, he did his chores, and he practiced Kabbalah. He would get up at various times each morning just to practice his spiritual prayers. Everyone in the house thought he was strange. But of course, when we assume things instead of just asking, we end up making fools of ourselves. Why do we do these things? When we assume things about others we eventually find a different truth. Kind of like God, right? Instead of assuming He's real or fake, or a mean God or a good God, we could just ask Him right?

Lots of things were said about this man. For example: it was said that every day he would pack his things up and go camping in the woods just because that was all he knew. After he felt more comfortable talking to me, he would later reveal to me that he went to the library every day because he was an avid reader. Who would have thought? During our many conversations we talked about the bible, the constitution, the founding fathers, slavery, presidents, and more. Most surprisingly he was an author as well. When he told me he had dreams of dying on the street because of his chosen lifestyle, even though I didn't agree and couldn't relate to him in that way, I completely understood it. We only get one life and how we chose to live it, be it God filled or not, is up to us. But why do we always believe what everyone else believes instead of forming our own opinions? Are you your own person who goes against the grain or are you just like everybody else?

Readers Notes: Was there ever a time when you were the woodsman? Have people assumed things about you? Most importantly do you assume a lot when it comes to God and his plans for you?

_____

_____

_____

_____

_____

_____

_____

_____

_____

_____

_____

_____

_____

A Moment of Reflection: Stop covering up for people who refuse to change or show genuine remorse. We can't force the people in our lives to change. Do you know that if people refuse to change, or refuse to work on how they treat you and continue to treat you wrong, that is called mistreatment and a form of abuse? Tell me about that one relationship where this may apply and what you intend to do about it.

_____

_____

_____

_____

_____

_____

_____

_____

_____

_____

_____

_____

_____

_____

The Power of Words and How They Can Either Heal or Destroy

Word Exercise: remember all the words that we highlighted in previous note sections? Go back to each positive and negative word, write each word down below and cross out the negative words. Pray for God to release those negative words from your body and give light and love to the positive words. Do you feel lighter?

_____

_____

_____

_____

_____

_____

_____

_____

_____

_____

_____

The Believer

Are You Living Your Best Life Right Now?

So we got through most of the guide. Now it's time to bring it all in and connect the dots. When My husband and I had decided to temporarily separate over some marital issues we had been having, I ended up hitting a huge wall. Just when you think you know God's plan for your life, one day when you least expect it, the hammer drops and suddenly you find yourself on your knees, sobbing, and asking God why me? Well, that's precisely what happened to me. After finding happiness, after giving birth to my second child, and having found my niche (Writing), it seemed as if everything was playing out perfectly. But beyond my knowledge, God was calling me to a higher level of purpose and responsibility. And of course, with that greater responsibility comes chastisement from our Lord and Savior. It was through my marital problems and separation where God not only began to use me but began calling me into ministry.

It doesn't seem ideal to start a ministry or any other project when your days are filled with crying, crazy emotions, a screaming baby, and trying to plan a separation. But that was exactly how it happened for me. God knew that I could handle it. That is exactly why people say, He won't give you more than you can handle. Not only was I very active in church, and taking on multiple ministries, I was also blessed to lead two life groups. So just when I thought I was living my best life, God came along and said "I have way more in store for you".

Do you feel like you're living your best life? Has God thrown a monkey wrench into your plans? Take some time to think about all your latest and current accomplishments. Do they fulfill you? And most importantly, do they align with God's purpose for your life? If you don't know what this feels like, or how to even begin the process of aligning yourself with God, proceed to the next chapter.

Prayer:

Father God, please reveal to me my true purpose in this life. I know that I have fallen off track and that I have allowed worldly and fleshly desires to get in the way of your plan for me. But I have gone back into my past, I have dug deep, and I have released all sins and pain to you. I ask for forgiveness again oh Lord, and I am ready to receive all that you may have in store for me. Amen!

Scripture of reference:

Delight yourself in the Lord and he will give you the desires of your heart. (Psalm 37:4)

Reader's Notes: Write Down your accomplishments and rate your satisfaction level on a scale of 0-10. Does anything stick out to you? It could it be your purpose?

_____

_____

_____

_____

_____

_____

_____

_____

_____

_____

_____

_____

_____

_____

_____

Freestyle chapter: Where do you see yourself I ten years?

_____

_____

_____

_____

_____

_____

_____

_____

_____

_____

_____

_____

_____

_____

_____

_____

Have You Ever Asked God About Your Purpose?

God is very intentional and time sensitive. Everything has its proper place and time, we just have to catch up to it. There's God's journey for our lives and then there's ours. God's journey is a straight path to our purpose in this life. For example: he already has everything set in place such as each destination stop, the people we will meet along the way, opportunities waiting to happen to get us to the next level and even our not so easy lessons, and so on and so forth. (I will touch more on this topic later)

Now, when we do things our way, our journey consists of pit stops, detours, and zig zags. This is the complete opposite of his path for us. What looks cleaner a straight line or a zig zag? What path seems easier to follow, a straight line or a zig zag? I know I would be out of breath losing steam and hope along the way trying to follow a zig zag pattern. Unfortunately, many of us end up taking our own route. We diverge from God's plan and that's where we begin to set ourselves up for pain, failure, and heartbreak. Now to say that God's journey for us will exclude lessons and pain would be dishonest, because it definitely won't, but there's a huge difference between his lessons and our own self-inflicted lessons.

God's goal is to constantly stretch us and mold us, not only as believers, but for our true purpose. And with these strategized lessons, not only is he on the other side waiting for us to get through them, as he coaches us from the sidelines, but these lessons will often be in place for a specific time and for a specific purpose. However, we do have an adversary. As soon as we come from the womb the enemy is already there waiting to ruin God's plan for our lives. One would probably ask, "Well why would the enemy be waiting for us as soon as we are born, to ruin God's plan and purpose for our lives?" Do you know that the enemy is in constant contact with God and our Lord and savior, trying to throw dirt on our names, trying to convince God that we are not worthy? But thanks to Jesus and his blood that covers all, He goes to bat for us every single time. The enemy doesn't want us in the knowing, he wants us lost and confused. That's one less believer helping to fight against his army.

One of our greatest examples in the Bible, is the story of Job. He was one of God's most loyal servants and he was used as a lesson, to show Satan how much God knows our hearts and how much God truly does love us and controls everything in both the spiritual realm and the earthly realm. God allowed the enemy to test Job's loyalty but with limitations. When God allows the enemy to test us, he gives the enemy specific instructions and limitations on how to do so. When we invite the enemy and his army into ourselves, we are no longer under God's instructions but under the consequences of our own actions and sin, giving the enemy a license to stick around for a lot longer, and to do more damage than we might be able to handle. (suicides, overdoses, murdering, diseases)

One would probably ask, "If God loves us why would he allow this to happen?" God is a sovereign God. He will never force us to do anything against our own will. He is a God of freewill. That is why it is important to know who He is, to learn his voice and to constantly seek him. The best way to combat the enemy and to make sure we are on the right course, is to stay in the word, and to simply ask Him, "God, what is your purpose for my life?" He will surely answer. Take some time to sit down with God, read His word, pray and ask Him about your purpose.

Prayer:

Father God, please give me the ability to realign myself with you. You are Alpha and Omega. The beginning and the end. What is my true purpose in this world? Through you all things are possible. Father God, please reveal to me my purpose. Please give me the steps I need to get the best results. Amen!

Scripture of reference:

And we know that God causes all things to work together for good to those who love God, to those who are called according to His purpose. (Romans 8:28)

Reader's Notes: Did God reveal your true purpose? Tell me what your purpose is!

_____

_____

_____

_____

_____

_____

_____

_____

_____

_____

_____

_____

_____

_____

_____

_____

Do You Believe in the Ministry Gifts?

Today in most churches, they tend to not teach or speak upon the spiritual gifts or the five-fold ministry (See below for further description). This is a huge disservice to not only the church and us believers, but to the world that looks to us as a light in the darkness. You can't pick and choose what you want to teach in the Bible or what you choose to believe. You either believe in all of it or none of it. Religion and the tradition of man has not only watered down the gospel but has left a sour taste in many people's mouths.

When you recite control, harsh judgment, false personas, and a holier than thou lifestyle, you begin to take the glory away from God and turn the glory onto man. God is about love, forgiveness, meekness, humility, and loving thy neighbor as thyself. If we truly want to start living for his glory, changing the way the world sees religion, and winning more souls, it is imperative that we get back to teaching the spiritual gifts and the five-fold ministry. By doing so we are allowing all to contribute to the body of Christ with our own unique styles and gifting.

Christ gave some to be apostles, some prophets, some evangelists, some preachers and some teachers. (Ephesians 4:11)

To one there is given through the spirit the message of wisdom, to another a message of knowledge, to another faith, to another gifts of healing, to another miraculous powers, to another prophecy, to another distinguishing of different spirits, to another speaking in different tongues, and to another the interpretation of different tongues. (For exact wording of scripture see 1 Corinthians 12)

For Many are called but few are chosen. (Matthew 22:4)

I believe that God has a purpose for each and every one of our lives. Now, whether or not we all get to achieve these purposes depends on not just the preacher and what he chooses to teach, but the individual as well. God has a plan for all of us and wants to save as many of us as possible. He will do whatever it takes to get our attention. He could use a storm, a life lesson, a death, a book, a person, place, or thing to get our attention. One of the amazing things about God is that he's always extending the olive branch. But eventually he will grow tired of trying to reach out. Unfortunately, many of us will push the limits of God forcing him to remove his hand from over our lives and leaving us to our own destruction.

With that being said, we all have a purpose in this life, and we are all born with many of the spiritual gifts listed. Your spiritual gifts should tie into your purpose. If you've found your purpose, finding your gifts should be easier. Or maybe you found your gifts first but are still trying to find your purpose. Either way they both are interconnected. Let's take a look at the five-fold ministry gifts (Apostles, prophet, evangelists, preacher, and teacher). These are all offices that some were born into but can take many years to obtain. These offices are called to a higher standard which can result in harsher punishment if not served correctly.

Not many of us have been called into an office but all of us have the spiritual gifts mentioned above. What are your spiritual gifts? Do you fit into a five-fold ministry office? Take some time to write some things down such as: what do I like to do? What are some of the things that people say I am good at? Do I like helping the sick? Do I like to teach? Sit and read up on the spiritual gifts and take your list to God for revelation and confirmation and he will make it known. Speak to your pastor for guidance on this topic.

Prayer:

Father God, what are my gifts? Please direct me and help me to figure out what spiritual gifts you have placed inside of me. Father God, I want to be a light in this dark world. Use me oh Lord and I will make you proud. Amen!

Scripture of reference:

God sent his only son into the world not to condemn the world but to save the world through him (John 3:17)

Reader's Notes: Write down your spiritual gifts or talents.

Taking a Leap of Faith

So now you know what your gifts are. After fasting, praying and speaking with your pastor and the Lord, what actions would he require you to take next? As I stated in my introduction, God used my marriage and separation to prepare me for ministry and my wilderness experience, this process would be a time of reflection, one on one time with God, facing my past demons, and ultimately studying his word. When God wants to use us, in order to make us brand new it requires a wilderness experience.

The wilderness experience truly depends on you. Now depending on your particular situation, how much you might have to learn, your ability to listen to God, and the particular call on your life, this will all determine the amount of time you stay in the wilderness. Even though it may be a painful season (God deals with us through seasons) or a difficult time in the wilderness, I can assure you that regardless of what you may face, not only will you come out tougher, stronger, and more knowledgeable, you'll become even more closer to Him than ever before.

How does God speak to us? God speaks to us in many ways mainly through the Holy Spirit. The Holy Spirit will often unction us when God is trying to get our attention. As we grow as believers, and as we develop more in His word, we can begin to hear God through inspired thoughts. Sometimes He may show us a word, or a number, or an image over and over again until we stop and begin to entertain those signs. Have you ever had a thought suddenly pop up into your head? Well a lot of times when we have these experiences, especially if the thought is something that we would never think of, it's usually the Lord trying to tell us something. But I caution every believer to be careful. We have three voices: we have our own voice, the enemy's voice, and that of the Lord's. To know for sure whose voice it is, line it up with scripture and if it goes against it, it's not God. God's word does not change.

In my twenty years of being a believer, I have come to the realization that in order to fully experience God you have to be a little out there. God is a spirit, and therefore he operates not only in the earthly realm but in that of the spiritual. You have to have an imagination and an open mind to see what cannot easily be seen. This also requires taking a leap of faith. After consulting with God of course, he may want you to quit that job. He might want you to move across the country. God can be very unconventional to get his glory and to get you to your purpose and goals. Yes, God has goals. The body of Christ is His main goal. The body (which consists of you and I) is like a never ending river. God uses us to replenish that river with nutrients. (New believers) by using the spiritual gifts, five-fold ministry, personal ministries and etc.

Prayer:

Father God, I am so scared. I do not know which way to go. What seems like the right path scares me and seems like the unimaginable. Please Lord shine your light on the correct path. The enemy has used many people and things to keep me from taking that jump. You are a good father who can defeat fear. Help me to release the fear oh Lord so that I can walk in your will. Amen!

Scripture of reference:

So do not fear for I am with you. Do not be dismayed, for I am your God. I will strengthen you and help you; I will uphold you with my righteous right hand. (Isaiah 41:10)

Reader's Notes: How will you reveal your gifts? Will you use them at church? At work? In the community? (These gifts along with your spiritual journey, should be discussed with your pastor)

_____

_____

_____

_____

_____

_____

_____

_____

_____

_____

_____

_____

_____

_____

Stepping into Purpose

(The Wilderness Experience)

The First Phase: (Isolation)

So, we talked about the premises of being a believer, right? We talked about the fact that we are all born with a purpose and with spiritual gifts. Our purpose and our gifts belong to God first and foremost. He must get the glory, for us to reap the rewards? The main reward of course is eternal life and getting to meet our Lord and Savior. Our main purpose is to replenish the river (The Body of Christ). We do this by casting our light into darkness and operating in our ministries to save souls. You answered the call. Everything seems to be flowing in the right direction. You've received revelation and confirmation from God and now you've hit a wall. This is called the season of the wilderness.

A year prior to my husband and I's separation, the Lord had warned me that it would happen. During a Five-hour drive heading home, I can remember sitting next to my husband after having a huge argument and telling him we were going to separate. He looked at me nonchalantly and said, "oh yeah?" About five months prior to our separation the lord spoke to me again regarding the split, this time pressing me to tell my husband that he was running out of time if things did not change.

This separation wasn't easy for me because not only do I love my husband, but I take my vows very serious. Parallel to my marriage going through some major changes, simultaneously, God had begun to call me into ministry. Now let's go back a few years prior while in my twenties. During my twenties the Lord told me that things would start happening once I hit thirty. Well, about three months before my thirtieth birthday, I received and answered the call to ministry. By the time I hit thirty, the Lord had started preparing me by sending me back home. What I thought would be me starting my ministry turned out to be me starting my wilderness process. See, everything about home was a representation of the wilderness. I'm talking temptation from past lovers, a lifestyle filled with materialistic things, dealing with toxic relationships with my mother figures, and my ex fiancé.

Once the wilderness process gets started, typically God isolates you from everything and everybody. You might stop going to church. You might stop hanging with your friends and family. You might even stop watching tv. God does this so that he can download information into you, grow stronger within you, and open your eyes to some issues. He also wants to help you achieve what he has in store for you. I know that this initial phase of the process might seem scary at first but trust me it is for your own benefit. God can spot a wolf posing in sheep's clothing. If God removes a person from your life, it's for a good reason.

The Second Phase: (Removing Generational Curses and Licenses)

Let's talk about the second phase. After isolation takes place everything around you will get crazy. Your finances become a mess. Your relationships go haywire. People start dropping in and out of your life for reasons you cannot explain. And you find yourself asking God why? Why is this happening?

When God wants us to grow in our faith, the wilderness process is used to tempt us with people and things we thought we had our grips on. Lessons from the past pop up, people you haven't spoken to in years pop up, and things get foggy. Can you handle this? Have you grown? Are you on the right track? Am I number one in your life? These are all questions that God begins to ask you. It feels like an intense pressure cooker. Pressure that makes you ask questions like can things get any worse?

Let's talk about those licenses shall we? Have you given the enemy a license to take dominion over your life? These licenses can stem from generational curses, an addiction, or perhaps something you may have done when you were younger that you didn't repent for. The enemy will use any door that has been left open in our lives, like unfinished business with a parent, to linger around to oppress and to demonize us. Do you have trouble sleeping at night? Do you feel like you are being watched? Have you faced a ton of demonic attacks from loved ones for no reason at all? This is called being demonized and oppressed.

Let's talk about realms. There's an earthly realm in which we dwell in, and then there's a spiritual realm in which God, the Lord, angels, and demons dwell in. In the spiritual realm there are laws. The enemy and his army cannot touch the Children of God unless he has been given permission to or the right to. These permissions or the "right" can come from either a license or from God himself. Again, look back to the story of Job for further example.

Have you ever had situations in your life where the same cycle just kept popping up? Or you had this certain mindset where you told yourself something was acceptable, like being with an abusive partner? Not only is that something that could be a generational curse, but that could be a license that was given to the enemy to keep you in that bondage and to keep you in that same abusive pattern. What do we do if we find ourselves in this situation? We repent and let God do his work.

During my wilderness experience God had shown me that I had some doors open from my past that needed to be closed. I also looked into my family's history and realized that there were lots of things passed down from generation to generation that posed as a problem and contributing factor to unhealthy patterns in my life. Once I realized this I began to pray and repent for my elders and went as far back as I could. I'm talking beyond my grandmother's generation, even beyond her mother's generation. I sincerely asked God for forgiveness. I asked for forgiveness for my ancestors and to free myself and my family from those curses. After a good forty minutes, I really felt a difference in the atmosphere and changes started taking place. I felt so much lighter. Research Generational curses. (Sexual abuse, sickness, addiction,) Do you think you suffer from some? What about your family? Research the Courts of Heaven for more information on freeing yourself of generational curses and licenses obtained by the enemy.

Reader's Note: (Begin to write about your wilderness experience)

_____

_____

_____

_____

_____

_____

_____

_____

_____

_____

_____

_____

The Third Phase: (Is it Them or is it Me?)

One of the hardest things in life can be admitting one's faults. This leads us to the third stage of the wilderness process: "Is it them or is it me?" During this stage God will bring back a person, be it a friend or family member, to reexamine the relationship. Are you holding onto a past hurt with this person? Have you had closure and have you forgiven this person? What role did you play in the demise or struggle of the relationship? And sometimes God will bring that connection back to the surface so you can slay that Goliath. (Reference 1 Samuel and 2 Samuel regarding the story of King David)

Yes, you read correctly. The Lord looks out for his children. That's why the bible tells us to love our enemies while allowing God to deal with them. We are not perfect, we are not God, so how can we take it upon ourselves to punish someone? We leave that process to God. But easier said than done right?

Scripture of reference:

When the Lord takes pleasures in anyone's way, he causes their enemies to make peace with them. (Proverbs 16:7)

If you listen carefully to what he says and do all that I say, I will be an enemy to your enemies and will oppose those who oppose you. (Exodus 23:22)

When I had initially spoke to my mother figure about the children and I coming to stay at her house during my separation, I knew that I was taking a chance. Given our long history of many ups and downs over the years, I knew I was taking a huge gamble. But with two children and struggling to catch up in life, I had no other options. At first the situation seemed like a clever idea and it seemed to be working out. But before I knew it, the enemy went rampant and the situation slowly begin to change for the worst. We started arguing over money, the children, cleaning, and noise in the house. Then it became more than just that. It suddenly went from arguing over toys to things that happened when I was in high school.

I wasn't and adult anymore. I wasn't Kristen Lory, who had a husband and two kids, I was now childlike. I was back in my old room during my high school days, where I would cry and where I had suffered from terrible depression. I was forced to relive verbal and emotional abuse all over again. Have you ever found yourself in a situation where you kept going back to a toxic person or place even though it was painful? You thought you dealt with it. You thought you were fine, but all it took was one situation to unfold and you were back in bondage.

To make the situation better, I started working. I even took on two jobs. I did this to not only have money, but to ensure that I would never have to move back home unless I wanted to. It seemed like my husband was waiting for me to fail because he wanted me back home. The enemy was pressing on all of my open wounds that had never healed over the years. Things had become very strained and tiring, pushing me toward burnout. Another part of the separation that I wasn't too happy about was the fact that I decided to step outside of my marriage during the separation. I was angry and needed any validation I could find, to help me feel better and to help me cope with my situation.

I believe that this person and situation was an isolated attack from the enemy. Why? Because this person was everything I ever wanted, but everything I should have run away from at the same time. I had made my husband fully aware of this situation, so I was very open, honest and truthful about it. I felt justified because of all of the things my husband had put me through. Let's just say we both committed a form of adultery. When we committed adultery within our marriage we committed adultery against God.

Where was the love that I had for myself? Where was my self-dignity? God really used that situation to anchor himself in me, because it was through that situation where I had begun the process of breaking that cycle of toxic and abusive relationships. This situation felt so good but was also very painful. I had to lean on God's voice to get me out of it and it took a while, but I eventually moved on. It wasn't easy, yet it was necessary for me to begin to see my worth.

Reader's Notes: Are you blaming others or holding grudges?

_____

_____

_____

_____

_____

_____

_____

_____

_____

_____

_____

_____

_____

_____

_____

The Fourth Phase: (Loss and Prevention)

The fourth phase of the wilderness is what I would like to call "Loss and Prevention." Let's talk about loss. During our journeys we form these friendships and bonds along the way, and we actually form soul-ties with these individuals. Did you know that a soul-tie isn't just connected to sex? A soul-tie can be a strong attachment to any person or situation where the bond is strong, or where something traumatic happened to us, making it hard to move forward. As I had stated earlier, during the wilderness process, God will touch on every area of your life, sometimes resulting in the loss of certain relationships.

While we are going through this phase it might seem painful. You may find that suddenly the people you thought were closest to you no longer talk to you. They don't respond if you contact them at all. And it leaves your mind boggled and confused. In my experience during this phase it was painful losing friends that I had known for years. But looking back now, those friends were either never really my friends or didn't believe in God. You can't take the past with you. Sometimes where God sends us there's no room for certain people.

After you've encountered loss, we begin to experience prevention. Once this happens the wilderness process begins to take a turn. The healing process as a whole begins to set in and suddenly, God starts to show you why he did what he did. After you lost that best friend of ten years, or after saying goodbye to your abusive parent for the final time, you suddenly see why it was a loss. The loss of those individuals or that toxic relationship, was not only to preserve you but to prevent you from stalling in your purpose.

Reader's Notes: Who or what have you been afraid to part ways with?

_____

_____

_____

_____

_____

_____

_____

_____

_____

_____

_____

_____

_____

The Fifth Phase: (Sharpening)

The healing process is now in effect. It was a crazy journey to say the least but you made it! After crying to the Lord, being forced to be at his feet, and leaning on his word to help get you through it, the sun has finally risen, and you feel nothing but his warmth and love. You feel renewed. You feel rejuvenated. Your eyes have been made brand new. The veil has been lifted and now you see the world with new eyes. This is the moment where you have truly arrived. Fantastic job!

Let's recap. Someway, somehow, either by a vision, by a dream, or through someone in ministry the Lord reached out to you asking if you were willing to answer the call (Ministry/Purpose). You said yes and suddenly, whether mentally or physically, he catapulted you into the wilderness and now everything is haywire. You've gone through the first few phases and now he wants to sharpen you, by going over everything you've just went through to iron out all the kinks. He might even throw in another test of temptation just to make sure you are done with old patterns and behaviors.

The Lord forces you to look at your role in all relationships past and present. And if he sees that progress has been made and lessons have been learned, he then begins to reveal his plans for you. We can't be preaching to the choir when we ourselves are a mess. We must be in alignment with his word and living righteously. Just when you thought you had him all figured out, he reveals his true purpose for you. He shows you his expectations when dealing with your gifts. And ultimately, he shows you his plans of how to get there. That is where the magic happens.

Butterfly (Release)

. Now that you have finished all five stages of the wilderness, it is now time for release. You should be feeling different. After experiencing gut wrenching lessons, pain, stretching, twisting, growing, and being healed by God, you should be in the process of living out your purpose. You should be on the right track and in alignment with God's purpose for your life.

As my wilderness experience ended, not only was I completely transformed, but I felt this wave of peace that never wavered. When we allow God to deal with us and when we allow him to transform our lives, we perceive everything differently. You no longer get mad at people or things like you used to. You no longer look to be the winner in an argument. You now know how to be the bigger person. You know how and when to let go. You learn to lean on the anchor that God places deep down inside of you, and you finally learn to give every single burden to him. Now get out there!

Readers Notes: Get out there and go! Write down your thoughts.

_____

_____

_____

_____

_____

_____

_____

_____

_____

_____

_____

_____

_____

_____

_____

The Power of Fasting and Prayer

Fasting and prayer are amazing tools that God has given us to strengthen our relationship with him. As believers it's something that we should be doing multiple times a year. When I first began fasting, I would use the first week of the month to fast. During the fast I would give up something like Facebook for example. To me, fasting doesn't have to necessarily be food, because if you have health issues like low blood sugar, you may need to use an alternative and God understands this.

After setting aside the first week of each month, I would sacrifice that one thing I couldn't do without and I would pick one book in the bible and study it, all while praying and asking God for revelation on the issues or areas in my life that needed the most guidance. When we fast, not only are we sacrificing something for God, but we are removing the chatter, studying his word, praying harder, and ultimately gaining wisdom, knowledge, revelation and confirmation.

Reader's Notes: Write about your fasting experiences.

_____

_____

_____

_____

_____

_____

_____

_____

_____

_____

_____

_____

_____

_____

_____

God's Timing

God's Timing is incredible. Right before my abrupt departure from my Mother figure's home, my husband and I had decided it was time to reconcile. I was so thankful to God for not only forgiving our sins, but for restoring our marriage. It took me a while to let go of that chapter of my life. Our separation was a tough process for me. It was filled with lots of anger, bitterness, guilt, highs and lows. But through the grace of God we made it.

Despite the negatives there's always a silver lining, especially when you keep God at the center. Not only had I become closer to him than ever before, but I slayed my Goliath. I was released from many generational curses, and ultimately learned how to love unconditionally. See, prior to separating I didn't really know what loving unconditionally meant, because I had never received that from my parents. I had been operating from a place of brokenness this whole time. All I knew was abuse. As I stated earlier in the book, my grandparents raised me for the first few years of my life and played key roles many years after, but it's not the same as the love from your parents.

Unconditional love is loving without conditions. My husband whose story I choose not to tell because it's his story, struggled with some things and committed adultery of his own. But instead of seeing the hurt, pain, and shame he was dealing with, all I could think about was my own pain. I cared about what my mother thought. I cared about what my friends thought. But forgot about my role not only as a wife and a mother but as a Christian. Being a believer has helped me see the world through God's eyes. A view filled with love, empathy, and compassion.

Once that curse lifted, that generational curse that wouldn't allow me to really love my husband, the enemy no longer had a license in that area of my life, and that finally gave me the ability to love freely. Once this happened, all of my anger subsided, and my walls came down. And just like that I was looking at my husband with new eyes and it felt like the first few months of our relationship all over again.

A Moment of Observation: I hope you are beginning to see the silver lining in your life and relationships. Is there someone who you are beginning to see with new eyes?

_____

_____

_____

_____

_____

_____

_____

_____

_____

_____

_____

_____

Reader's Notes: Are things beginning to fall into place? Tell me about it.

_____

_____

_____

_____

_____

_____

_____

_____

_____

_____

_____

_____

_____

_____

Know your Purpose in God's Kingdom and Serve to the Best of your Ability

So now we are at the end of our journey. Excellent job. The process wasn't easy, but it was worth it. Let God use you and be a light in this world of darkness. Just think of not only the spiritual rewards (Eternal life), but the emotional rewards as well. We cried a bit, we got angry and we really dug deep, but we did it. Remember, we only get one life to live. Stand up in confidence and begin to operate in your purpose even when it hurts. Whether you're an entrepreneur, a teacher, an aspiring pastor and more, just remember that God's got this!

It is now time to be an asset to the kingdom of God. You have been transformed and you have been made brand new. You have either totally healed or are beginning to heal. But either way you are ready to get out there. We all see God differently. We all see church, tradition, and religion differently. We all worship differently but we all have a common goal and that Goal is to be happy while serving the Lord with all our might.. God loves us all the same. We are his chosen people. And he wants us to be happy.

I need you to be honest with yourself right here, right now, and ask yourself these questions. Have I truly been open to God throughout the years? Have I been blocking the blessings he might have had for me all this time? What can I do starting today to make my relationship with God better? If we can answer these questions truthfully and make a commitment today, to start allowing God to work in our lives, I promise you things will turn around for the better. The changes might not be immediate, and they might not be that big, but peace will come. I believe the results depend on you and how much you are willing to sacrifice and give God in return. Attending a church and getting involved in a ministry can be a great start. Being a part of a church family provides a sense of community and support from other believers.

What will your contribution be? Cast your light, love and knowledge onto the world. You have chosen to make the Lord absolute ruler over your life and you have given him complete dominion over your life. No devil or no other individual can take this from you. If you want to teach and preach, then teach and preach. If you want to evangelize than evangelize. Start that ministry that's been sitting on the backburner all these years. Go and start that business. Today we take a stand by never sitting on our dreams again. Thank you for allowing me into your personal space and thank you for going on this journey with me. You have become a butterfly so fly away and help change the world through God's eyes.

Find a Scripture that Speaks to Your Soul the Most and Write it Down Here.

Reader's Journal

(One month of entries for a time of self-reflection)

First Week: (Since Completing the Guide, What Have You Learned?)

_____

_____

_____

_____

_____

_____

_____

_____

_____

_____

_____

_____

_____

_____

_____

_____

_____

_____

_____

Second Week :(Write About Areas of Growth.)

Third Week: (Have you seen an Improvement in Your Relationship with God?)

Fourth Week: (Bring Your Purpose Into Perspective.)

Amen!

Made in the USA
Columbia, SC
17 December 2022